Collins

THE RET FRANKIE STINE

BARRY HUTCHISON

CHAPTER 1

Frankie woke up, flat on his back on a hard wooden board. He had a banging headache. That was the first thing he noticed. The second thing he noticed was that he was dead.

He wasn't sure how he knew exactly; he just did. There was that headache for one thing, and a strange "deady" sort of taste in his mouth for another.

There was a deathly stillness where his heartbeat should have been. He had never really noticed his heart beating before, but now that it wasn't, he was suddenly very aware of the empty silence in his chest.

And then, of course, there was the hand.

The hand wasn't his. The fingers were thick and sausage-like. The skin on the knuckles was scarred and rough. It was a hand built for hitting things, and Frankie had never hit anyone in his life.

The arm wasn't his, either. It was hairier than any arm he had ever seen, with a faded tattoo of a dragon wrapped around it. Neat black stitches criss-crossed the skin above the elbow and above the hand.

The other arm was not much better. It was slightly longer, slightly thinner and much less hairy. The fingers were long and tapered, with long nails that had turned a nasty shade of black at the tips.

The arms lay on top of a dirty grey sheet, which covered him from just below the neck down. The outline of his body beneath the sheet looked bulkier than normal, but he decided he could worry about that in a minute. One thing at a time.

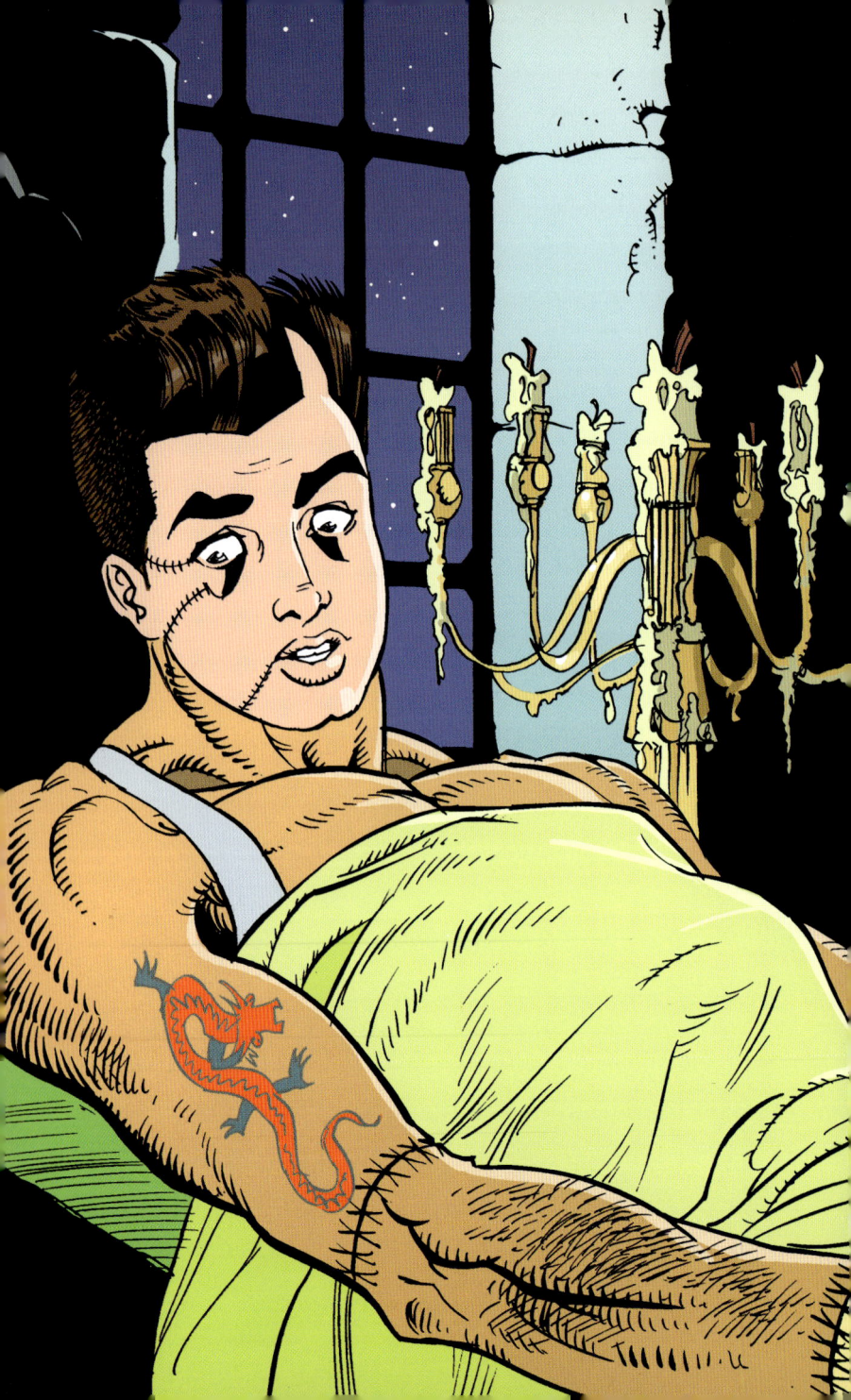

He balled both hands into fists and watched all his fingers flex in and out. The arms may not have been his originally, but they clearly belonged to him now. He wasn't really sure how he felt about that.

In fact, he wasn't really sure how he felt about anything at the moment. There was a fuzziness in his head like a thick fog. It made thinking quite tricky.

Frankie closed his eyes and tried to force his brain to work properly. What was the last thing he remembered?

He remembered breakfast – cornflakes with slightly sour-tasting milk that probably should have been tipped down the sink the day before. Could that have killed him? Death by milk poisoning?

Probably not.

He remembered the journey to school – sitting in the back seat while his mum and dad argued up front. There had been … something. A sudden screeching of brakes. A blasting of the horn.

Had he been in a crash?

No, because he remembered getting to school and being bored stupid in Maths. Perhaps that had been it. Had he literally been bored to death by Mr Brown's equations?

It was possible, but then he started to remember other things, too. His school lunch. The walk home. That piano falling on him. The ...

Wait.

Back up.

The piano. Yeah, that was probably it.

He remembered walking past the fancy new houses that had just been built along Stumm Street. He remembered the frantic shouts from the workmen above. He remembered looking up to see a grand piano grow larger and larger in the space above his head. And then ...

And then nothing.

So that was it. He had been crushed to death by a falling piano at the age of fifteen. That, Frankie decided, was just typical of his luck.

He was being very calm about the whole thing. He had noticed that. He would have expected to be screaming and panicking by this point, and yet he felt quite at peace. He was probably in shock, and any moment now he would …

"WAAAAAAARGH!"

Yep, there it was – full-scale terror came crashing down on him, in much the same way as that piano had.

His scream sounded like crunching gravel, all rough and hoarse and not like his usual voice at all. He tried to sit up, but something was fastened across his chest, pinning him to the board.

His new hands grabbed for the dirty sheet and yanked it away. Frankie looked down at himself, and could not believe what he saw.

CHAPTER 2

Frankie's body looked like a badly-made jigsaw of different parts, all held together with hundreds of little black stitches. He was wearing a vest and boxers that may once have been white, but were now a grubby shade of grey. He didn't recognise those either. As if things weren't bad enough, he was wearing someone else's underwear.

His skin came in a range of colours, none of them nice. His left leg was an angry purple, his right a deathly shade of grey. The other bits were yellowy-green mixed in with shades of brown.

His feet were different sizes. Even worse, they seemed to be on the wrong legs, so the big toes on each foot were on the outside. His toenails could seriously do with a trim, too.

He was in a small rectangular room with exposed stone walls and an arched wooden door.

There was a single window. Rain hammered against it, as if trying to come in from the darkness outside.

The room was lit by a few dozen candles that had melted away to waxy stumps. The light they gave off was dim and flickering, and cast spooky shadows across the walls.

"H-hello?" Frankie said. "Is … is anyone there?"

A flash of lightning lit up the dark sky outside as the door was thrown wide open. "It's alive!" cried a voice from the doorway.

A short, skinny man was hunched there, his eyes bulging excitedly. His body was stooped and bent. He hid it beneath a long white coat he kept buttoned right up to the neck.

His hair was wiry, grey and out of control, but the grin on his face revealed teeth that had been polished to perfection.

"Well bless-a my soul, I actually did it," said the man. His voice was deep and American, and not what Frankie had been expecting at all.

The voice reminded him of a singer his mum always listened to. Elvis something-or-other.

"Um … hello," said Frankie, and the grin fell from the man's face.

"Hey, wait just a minute," the man drawled. "You talked."

"What happened to me?" Frankie asked. "What have you done to me?"

The man slapped himself on the forehead. "Darn. I forgot the mind wipe," he muttered. "I swear, I'd forget my head if it weren't screwed on tight."

He hobbled over to where Frankie was lying, then ducked down out of sight. When he stood up again, the man was holding what looked like an electric drill, with three long needles bunched together at the front.

"The bad news is, this is *really* gonna hurt, son," he said. A wicked grin crept across his face. "The good news is that in sixty seconds time, you ain't gonna remember a single thing about it."

CHAPTER 3

Frankie tried to roll away, but the strap across his chest held him pinned.

"Wait, stop!" he pleaded, as the needles crept closer. "W-who are you? Why are you doing this?"

"Name's King. Professor Alvin King," the man said. "And I'm doing this because I can. If I can bring back one dead guy, I can bring back others. Bring back enough and I'll have an army, and no one on Earth can stand in my way."

Alvin brought the needle device closer to Frankie's face. "But first things first. Hold still while I stick these in your eye, son, and all those memories of yours will be a thing of the past."

"Leave me alone!" Frankie boomed. He sat up, snapping the leather strap in half.

Frankie's hulking right arm lashed out. Alvin's needle device smashed against the rough stone wall and fell in pieces to the floor.

"Now look what you've done," Alvin grumbled. "Those things don't grow on trees, you know."

Frankie stumbled on his muddled-up feet towards the door. There was a *clack* from behind him. He looked over his shoulder to see the professor loading a rifle.

"This knock-out dart will send an elephant to sleep for a month," Alvin explained. "Now, I don't much want to shoot you, son, so stand there or ..."

Frankie lunged for the door handle. He wasn't in full control of his body yet, though, and instead of opening the door he crashed straight through it. To his surprise, he staggered out into a neatly decorated corridor.

Doors lined the walls, each with a little brass number attached to the front.

At the far end of the corridor, an old lady in a green coat was waiting for a lift. The whole floor shook beneath Frankie as he lumbered towards her.

"Wait!" he bellowed. "Hold the lift!"

The old woman looked up. Her jaw dropped open. She began to jab her finger hurriedly at the buttons.

"Get back here, man. Don't make me shoot you!" shouted Alvin.

Frankie kept running. He thundered along the corridor, closer and closer to the woman by the lift.

"You asked for this!" yelled the professor. The rifle gave a sharp *crack*. Frankie stumbled sideways just as something went *thwip* through the air beside him.

Up ahead, the old woman toppled forwards into the lift as its doors opened.

"Now look what you made me do," shouted Alvin. "You made me shoot that old lady."

"Leave me alone, you nutter!" Frankie yelled. The lift was only a few metres ahead of him now. He was almost there. Almost free!

PING.

The lift doors slid closed just before he got there. Frankie let out a cry of fright as he saw the full horror of his reflection in the polished metal.

The face was the only part he recognised, although even that was criss-crossed with stitches and looked too small for his body. The rest of him had changed drastically.

He stood a good six-and-a-half feet tall, much taller than he had been before. His chest and shoulders bulged with knotted muscles. They looked as if someone had nicked them from the world's strongest man. A line of stitches circled his neck, attaching his head to the rest of the body.

No wonder the old woman hadn't held the lift door open for him. He was a monster.

"End of the road, son," drawled Alvin, slipping another dart into the chamber of the rifle. "Ain't nowhere left to run."

Frankie's eyes darted left and right. There were no doors down that end of the corridor. Apart from the lift, the only escape was past the professor and his gun.

"You belong to me. I made you," Alvin said.

He raised the rifle, closed one eye and took aim. In that moment, Frankie knew exactly what he had to do. He had just one chance.

Spinning on his heels he dug his fingers into the gap between the lift doors and heaved. There was a *screech* as the metal buckled, revealing a drop into sheer darkness beyond.

Frankie stared into the gloom. "What's the worst that can happen?" he whispered through gritted teeth. "I'm already dead."

Somewhere behind him, the rifle went *crack*. A sharp pain stung at Frankie's shoulder.

And he jumped down into the dark.

CHAPTER

The air in the lift shaft was warm and stuffy. The smell of oil and grease swirled up Frankie's nostrils as he plunged down, down, down through the gloom.

He seemed to fall forever. He had just started to think he should have hit something solid by now, when he hit something solid. He landed with a *boom* on the roof of the lift. Jolts of pain shot up his legs and through his spine, making his teeth rattle inside his skull.

A yelp of relief burst from his lips. He might be hurting, but at least he wasn't dead. No more dead than he had been a few moments ago, anyway.

"You better not have broken up that body, son," shouted Alvin, leaning through the buckled doorway, the rifle in his hands.

Frankie ducked into the shadows and held his breath, waiting until Alvin had vanished back through the hole.

Carefully, he felt his shoulder until he found the dart. It was buried deep in his flesh, just the feathery tail sticking out. Frankie bit down on his lip and pulled the dart free. There was a tingling at the base of his skull, but other than that the professor's poison didn't seem to be having much effect. So much for being able to stop an elephant.

Frankie had just started to wonder how he was going to get out of the lift shaft when a teenage girl stepped out of the wall, nearly making him jump out of his skin in fright. Not that he would really have minded, what with his skin being so horrible.

She was smaller than he had been even when he was alive, and dressed in a pink jogging suit. When she saw Frankie, her eyes widened just a little in horror and surprise.

"Yikes! You're worse than I thought," she said. Then she added, "No offence," as an afterthought.

"How did you get in here?" Frankie gasped.

"I didn't. I'm not really here," said the girl. "And you shouldn't be either. You need to get out."

She pointed down to the roof of the lift right beneath them. "There's a hatch. Open it," the girl commanded. "Dig your fingers in and pull."

There was a sharp squeal of bending metal as Frankie dug in his fingers and pulled. Instead of the hatch opening, the entire corner of the roof lifted up like the lid of a tin can.

"Or just tear the whole roof open," said the girl. "Whatever works. Now go. I'll meet you out the front."

With a swirl of pink light she vanished. A moment later, she appeared again. "Sorry, should have said. *Hurry up!*"

CHAPTER 5

Frankie dropped through the hole into the lift below. The old woman was still lying flat on her back, snoring gently and muttering something about cabbages.

The lift doors were making no attempt to open, so Frankie wedged his fingertips into the gap and heaved them apart.

He found himself in a hotel lobby. Twenty or more people milled about, checking in, chatting, or sipping expensive coffees.

They all stopped and stared when Frankie tore open the door.

"Um … hi," said Frankie, giving a little wave.

As if on cue, everyone in the foyer began to scream.

"M-monster!"

"What is that thing?"

"He killed that old woman!"

Frankie stepped from the lift, his hands held up in surrender. "No, wait. It wasn't me," he said, but no one was listening to him now. Some ran screaming into the street. Others took cover behind chairs and tables. A few brave souls approached him, fists raised, ready to fight.

From all around the lobby came shouts.

"Get him!"

"Call the police!"

"I think I just wet myself!"

The girl Frankie had seen in the lift shaft ducked under the approaching men and darted to Frankie's side.

"You made it," she said with a grin. "Sadly, many of these people now want to kill you – even though you're already dead. I suggest we escape. You in?"

Frankie nodded. "I'm in."

"That's the spirit," said the girl. She placed a hand on his arm and whispered something below her breath. There was a flash of light so bright it forced Frankie to screw his eyes shut tight. He felt something rush past him and a deafening roar filled his ears.

CHAPTER 6

The next thing Frankie knew, he was face down in a puddle with the rain battering against his back and the wind howling around him.

Frankie coughed and spluttered as the icy-cold liquid flooded his nose and throat. Arms shaking, he tried to push himself clear of the murky water.

With a roar of effort, he rolled onto his back and gasped for air. The girl stood over him, peering down, her head cocked to one side.

"You can't drown," she said. "You do know that?"

The cold water on Frankie's face was helping to clear the last few wisps of fog from his head. "C-couldn't breathe," he mumbled.

"Of course you couldn't breathe. You're dead," the girl said. "You can't drown, you don't breathe, you don't feel pain."

"I do feel pain," Frankie said. "The dart hurt. So did landing on that lift."

"Only because you expected it to," the girl said. "You didn't really feel it. It's all in your mind."

"I don't believe that."

The girl shrugged. "Suit yourself."

Frankie propped himself up on his elbows. "Who are you, anyway?"

"Megan Mogg, level two witch," said the girl. She reached into her pocket and produced a leather wallet. It dropped open, revealing a shiny badge and ID card. "And agent of SPOOK."

CHAPTER 7

Frankie heaved himself to his feet and examined the badge.

"You're a *witch*…" he said, "called *Megan Mogg*?" Frankie snorted. "That's the most ridiculous thing I've ever heard."

Megan looked offended. "You're a stitched-together dead guy called *Frankie Stine*," she pointed out. "If anyone's ridiculous here, it's you. Besides," she sniffed, "at least my feet are the right way round."

Frankie looked down at his feet, and remembered he was wearing nothing but underwear that was dangerously close to turning see-through in the rain.

"Clothes," he mumbled. "I need clothes."

"Done," said Megan. She clicked her fingers, and Frankie suddenly found himself squashed into a long green dress that puffed out at the waist. "Um, no, wait," Megan said, and she blushed slightly.

She clicked her fingers again. The dress was replaced by a set of grey overalls. A pair of work boots appeared on the ground right beside Frankie.

"Probably best if you stick them on yourself," Megan said. "You know, with your feet being so horribly messed up and everything."

"Gee, thanks," Frankie spat. He wrestled his feet into the boots – left foot in the right one, right one in the left.

Megan had taken cover in a nearby doorway. Frankie lumbered over and squeezed into the gap beside her.

"So," he began. "You're really a witch?"

"I really am."

"Shouldn't you be wearing a hat or carrying a broomstick or something?"

"Yes. If I was five years old," she said. "And it was Hallowe'en."

The glare of car headlights swept across the alleyway. Megan slunk back into the shadows of the doorway. Frankie tried to do the same, but he was too big, so he stood very still and pretended to be invisible instead.

It wasn't until the car had passed that Megan spoke again. "You may be in trouble," she said.

Frankie gestured down at his hand-stitched new body. "You don't say."

"King is going to be looking for you. He's going to want you back."

"How do you know all this stuff?" asked Frankie.

"I told you, I'm an agent of SPOOK."

"So what does SPOOK stand for?" Frankie asked.

Megan squared her shoulders. "It stands for justice!"

Frankie rolled his eyes. "I meant, what do the letters stand for?"

"What do you mean?"

"SPOOK," said Frankie. "What do the letters stand for?"

"They don't stand for anything," said Megan. "It's just a name. You know, like FBI or whatever."

"FBI stands for Federal Bureau of Investigation," said Frankie.

Megan frowned. "Really? Well, like CIA then."

"Central Intelligence Agency."

"Oh right, fine," Megan said with a tut of annoyance. "Then it stands for Supernatural Police Officers ... um ... OK?"

Frankie fought back a grin. "*Supernatural Police Officers OK?*" he snorted. "That's who you work for? *Supernatural Police Officers OK?*"

"Look, do you want our help or not?" Megan demanded. "Because if not, I'll magic you back into that hotel and leave you to get on with it."

Frankie mimed zipping his mouth closed and gave Megan an encouraging nod.

"Right," she said. "So … you're dead, but you already figured that out. You died in a …"

"Piano accident," Frankie said.

For a moment there was no sound but the rattle of the rain on the pavement. "That was no accident," Megan said. "You were chosen."

"Chosen?" whispered Frankie. "You mean …?"

"That's right, Frankie," Megan nodded. "You didn't die in an accident. You were murdered!"

CHAPTER 8

Frankie felt as if his head was spinning again. This was rapidly turning into the worst day ever, second only to the day when he'd accidentally called his teacher "Mum" in front of the whole class. Mr Wilson really hadn't been happy about that.

"Murdered?"

Megan nodded. "That's right. You and half a dozen others."

Frankie felt his throat go dry. "By that King guy?"

Megan nodded again. "We've been closing in on him for months."

Megan pointed along the alleyway to where it opened out onto a city street. A towering building stood a block or two away. The word "Hotel" shone in white neon down its side.

"That's where you just came from. Third floor," said Megan. "Even now SPOOK agents are closing in on his room, and King doesn't suspect a ..."

KA-BOOM!

Frankie covered his ears as the entire third floor of the hotel blew outwards in an explosion of fire and smoke. Flaming chunks of rubble fell like meteorites to the ground, igniting the fuel tanks of cars parked below. They launched into the air like fireworks. Even from this distance, Frankie could hear the screams of people on the street.

With a low groan the bottom half of the hotel seemed to swallow up the floors above it. Then, with a final roar of shattering stone, the entire building went down in a choking cloud of dust and smoke.

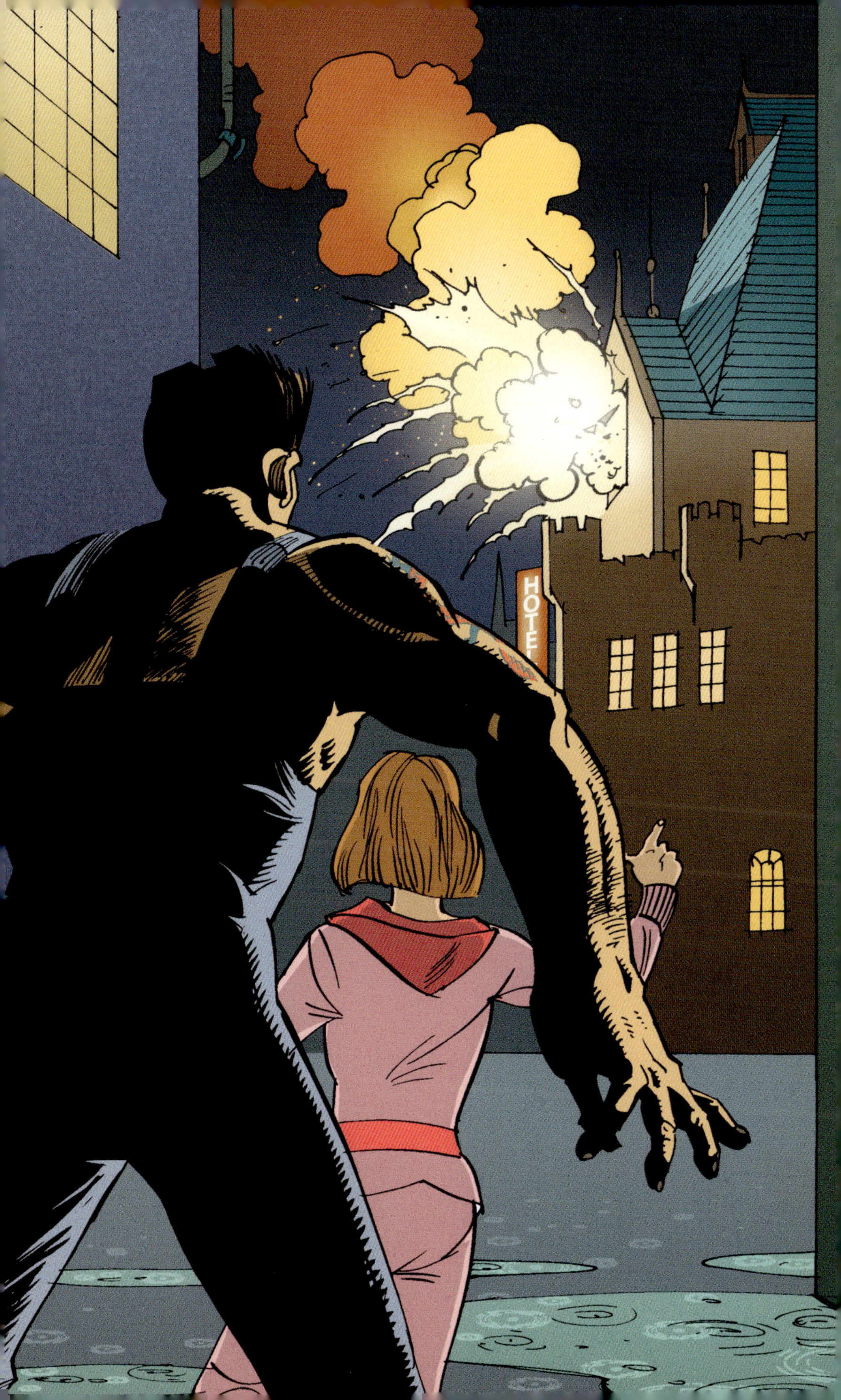

CHAPTER 9

The dust came rolling like a sandstorm towards them. Frankie turned and squashed himself into the doorway, using his hulking body to shield Megan until the cloud had carried on past.

A deep stillness fell, broken only by distant screams and the wailing of sirens. The alley was blanketed in a carpet of dust. Frankie's boots left deep imprints as he stumbled out of the doorway and looked at where the hotel had been.

"They … they blew him up?" he said. "Wasn't that a bit extreme?"

"N-no," said Megan, although she didn't look very sure. "They wouldn't. He must have blown himself up. He must have known they were coming, so he blew himself up."

Frankie frowned. "If he knew they were coming, why not just escape?"

"What?"

"I mean, if I was an evil scientist and I knew I was about to be arrested, I'd make my getaway before the cops turned up."

Megan's face went pale. "You're right. He wouldn't blow himself up." She grabbed Frankie by the arms and turned him to face her. "Where would you go," she demanded, "if I wasn't here?"

Frankie didn't need to think about the answer to that one. "Home," he said.

"Then that's where King will go," she said. "The explosion was just to cover his tracks."

Even though it wasn't beating, Frankie could have sworn he felt his heart start to race. "But my parents. King's a killer! We have to get there before him," Frankie cried. "We have to stop him!"

Megan nodded. "We will."

"How? He's got a head start. We'll never catch him on foot."

"Who said anything about going on foot?" Megan asked.

"You can magic us there?" asked Frankie, hopefully.

Megan shifted uneasily on her feet. "Um, no. Not exactly. But I can do the next best thing."

CHAPTER 10

Frankie stood at the side of the road, the rain plastering his hair to his face.

"A bus?" he muttered. "This is your great plan? A bus!"

"SPOOK won't cover taxi costs," Megan said. A convoy of emergency services vehicles screamed past in the direction of the collapsed hotel. "But don't worry, this is no ordinary bus!"

"Can it fly?" Frankie asked.

"Well no, but it's a double-decker, so that's pretty exciting," said Megan. She caught the stunned expression on Frankie's face. "Are you still thinking about your parents being killed?"

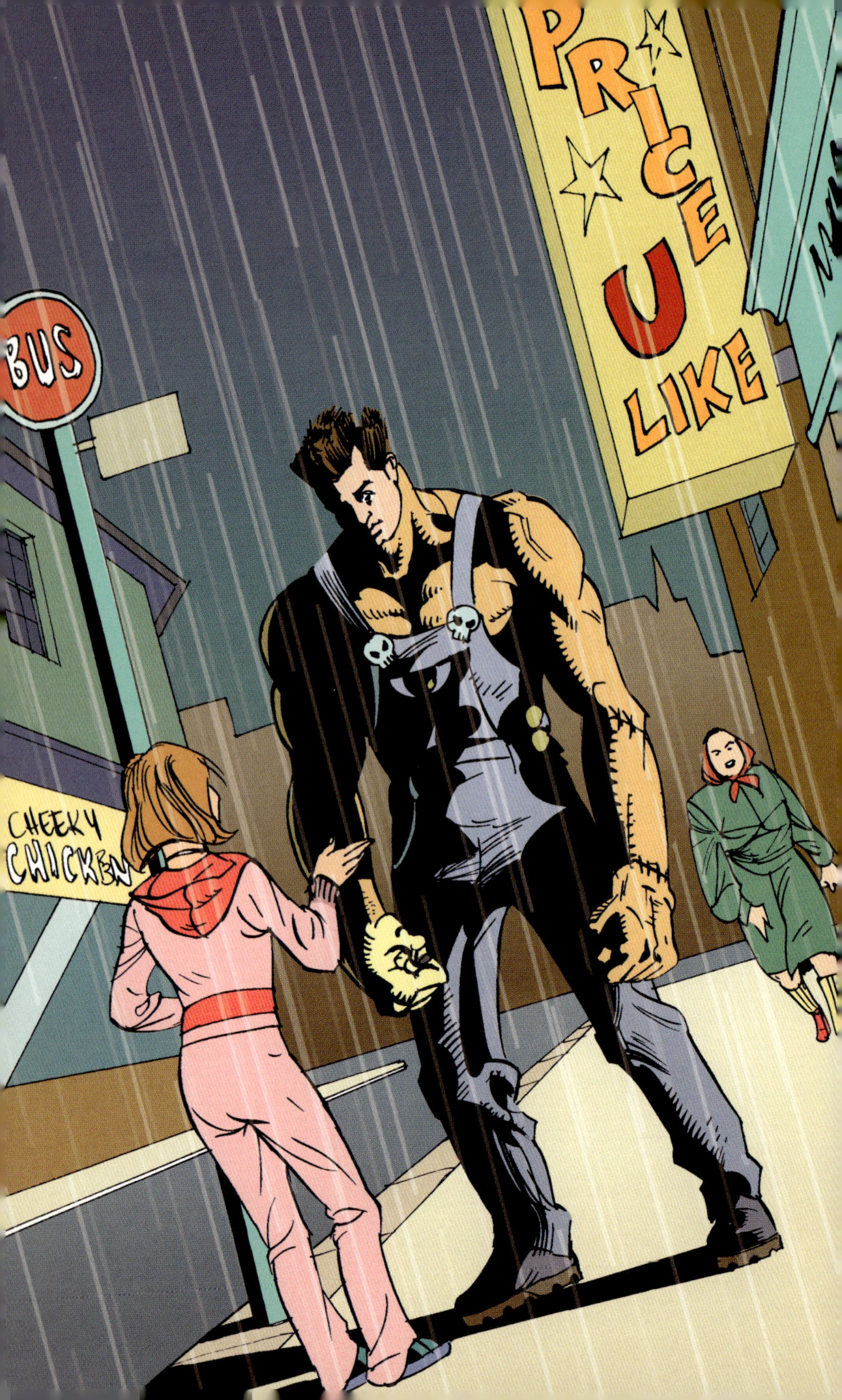
PRICE U LIKE
BUS
CHEEKY CHICKEN

"Yes, I'm still thinking about my parents being killed!" Frankie snapped. He felt hot tears spring to his eyes. "He'll catch them off guard. They'll still be in mourning."

"What about?" Megan asked.

"Well, about me dying, I'd have thought!"

Megan blinked. "Oh, yeah," she said. She cleared her throat. "There's something I should tell you ..."

"Bus," said Frankie. A double-decker trundled around the corner towards them.

Megan rummaged in her pockets and produced a handful of change. She counted it out just in time for the bus to chug on past in a cloud of diesel fumes.

"Out of service," said Frankie, reading the sign above the bus's door.

Megan tutted. "Yeah, I did wonder about that," she said. "You know, with the whole building exploding everywhere thing? They must be shutting down the roads."

"Then you have to magic us there. Teleport us or whatever. Like you did in the lift shaft."

Megan shook her head. "Can't. Too dangerous. I knew exactly where I was going that time. I'd already scoped out the alleyway. If I try to take us to your house, we might end up buried in a wall, or half-way through your dad."

"So what do we do?" cried Frankie. He was frantic with worry now.

"Don't worry, I have an idea," Megan said. She looked up and down the street. "First, I just need to find a post box."

CHAPTER 11

The streets were deserted. Everyone had either gone running away from the explosion, or was hiding under their bed.

Megan glanced along the street in both directions as she went towards a red post box at the side of the road. She peeped through the letter slot and began to tap her fingers on both sides of the metal cylinder.

"What are you doing?" Frankie whispered.

"Ssh," Megan hissed. "Concentrating."

She tapped a few more times on the post box, then pressed both hands flat against its curved sides. A cool blue light lit up inside the letter slot and passed across Megan's eyes.

"Retina scan confirmed," chimed a robotic voice from inside the post box. "Agent Mogg identified."

With the faintest of clicks, a section of the road folded in on itself like a trapdoor, revealing a dark space beyond. As Frankie watched, something small and sleek on a moving platform rose up through the hole.

It had four chunky tyres and a curved metal bonnet. Where the roof should have been was a bubble of glass, like a giant fly's eye, making it look like a cross between a sports car and an insect.

The glass slid back as Megan approached, revealing two leather seats, a steering wheel, and about ten thousand flashing lights inside.

"Hop in," Megan told him.

With some effort, Frankie squeezed himself into the passenger seat. It was a tight fit, and his knees were pinned against his chest.

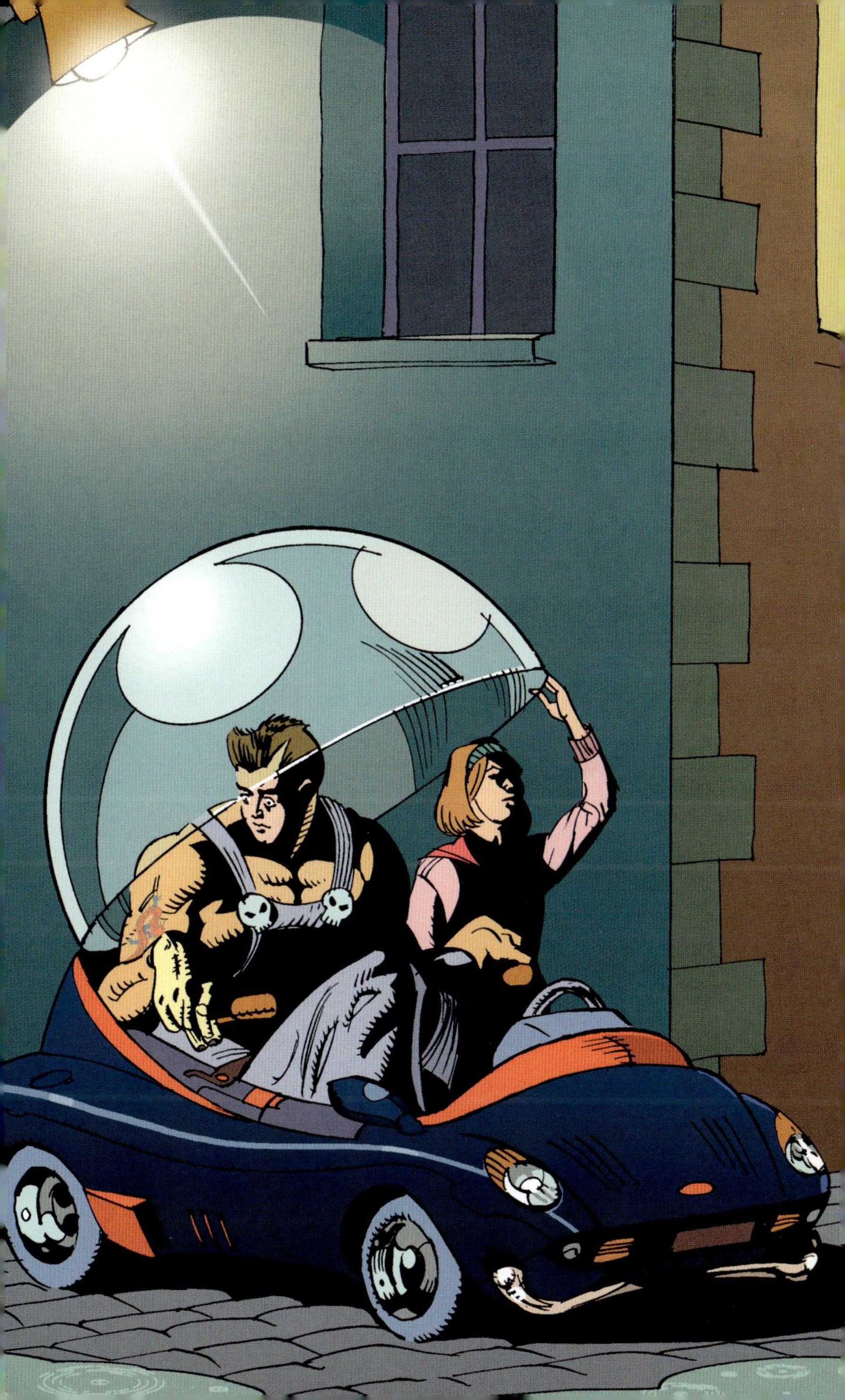

"Cool, huh?" Megan said. She flicked a switch and the glass roof slammed shut above them. "SPOOK emergency transport."

With a push of another button, the engine purred into life. Three computer screens blinked on around them. The darkened glass bubble also became a display. Lines and lines of information rolled past as the system booted up.

"Wait a minute, you're like, thirteen," Frankie said. "You're not old enough to drive a car."

"You're right, I'm not," Megan said. She jabbed another button. "Luckily, this is an aeroplane. We call it the Dragonfly."

With a *swoosh* and a *click*, four thin black wings unfolded from the sides of the vehicle. Its engines whined and the Dragonfly began to rise off the ground. It climbed steadily for a few metres, then swung sideways and headed for the nearest wall.

Megan wrestled with the wheel, fighting to get the vehicle back under control.

Frankie swallowed nervously as the building outside loomed closer and closer. "You have sat your pilot's test, right?" he asked.

"*Sat*? Yes," said Megan. "*Passed*? No."

"Danger! Danger! Obstacle detected!" screeched a voice from somewhere in the control panel. "Engaging automatic avoidance system."

The Dragonfly swung in a sharp semi-circle, pinning them to their seats. There was a *whirring* noise from below the jet and the voice from the console came again.

"Rocket thrusters engaged."

Frankie frowned. "Rocket thrust—" he began, then the rest of his sentence was drowned out by the roar of high-powered jet engines, and his own high-pitched screams of terror.

CHAPTER 12

Frankie felt as if his eyes were being shoved back into his head. The Dragonfly was racing across the sky at an impossible speed, punching through low clouds and streaking above high rooftops.

Muscles straining, he managed to turn his head enough to look at Megan. The Dragonfly was moving so fast her cheeks were being pushed back somewhere around her ears.

"This … is … brilliant!" she cried.

"Brilliant?" Frankie whimpered. "It's horrible!"

"Automatic avoidance system disengaged," chimed the voice from the console. The Dragonfly came to an abrupt stop in mid-air. The sudden slowdown threw Frankie and Megan forward in their seats, then slammed them back.

"Brilliant!" cheered Megan. "Shall we go again?"

"Only if you want me to throw up on you," Frankie said. "Anyway – my parents, remember?"

"Okay, okay," Megan grumbled. "Keep your stitches in." She studied the dashboard. Hundreds of little lights blinked back at her. Frankie watched her, getting more impatient with each second that passed.

"What are you waiting for?"

"Looking for the button," Megan said.

"What button?"

"Dunno. I'll know it when I see it. Something that'll let me steer again. It's locked, look."

She pushed forward on the steering wheel and Frankie gripped the armrests in panic. The Dragonfly, though, didn't move.

"This is it," said Megan. She pressed a button. A little door slid open in the dashboard and a metal hand came out to offer her a packet of travel mints. "OK, maybe it isn't."

"Do you even know what you're doing?" Frankie asked. "Have you flown one of these before?"

"Of course I have!" Megan said. "Well the simulator, anyway."

Frankie felt the veins in his head stand out like little ropes. "The *simulator*? You mean you've never flown a real one?"

Megan shook her head. "Technically, I shouldn't even be in it without a trained superior officer."

"We're so going to die," Frankie groaned.

"Relax," Megan replied. "You're already dead, remember?"

Frankie turned away and gazed out through the darkened glass. If he pressed his face against it, he was able to see the city below. He could make out the cars weaving through the streets. He could see a play park. Over there to the left was the start of the river, and further along on the right was …

"My school," Frankie said. "That's my school. But that means …"

He bounced in his seat, making the Dragonfly rock sideways in the air.

Before it rolled back upright, he saw the whole neighbourhood spread out before him. The school. The shops. The houses. *His* house.

"We're here," he said. "My house is right below!"

"Really?" Megan spluttered. "Er, I mean, yes. Of course it is. I had it all under control from the start."

"Then take us down," Frankie commanded.

"Um … that isn't going to be a problem," Megan said, but there was something about her voice that made Frankie turn to look at her.

Her eyes were wide and her hair was standing on end. She pointed at a monitor just as the voice from the console began to speak again. "Incoming missile detected. Automated avoidance system …"

But it was too late. Before the Dragonfly could move, a missile slammed into it from below, and the sky was lit by a bright, blinding ball of fire.

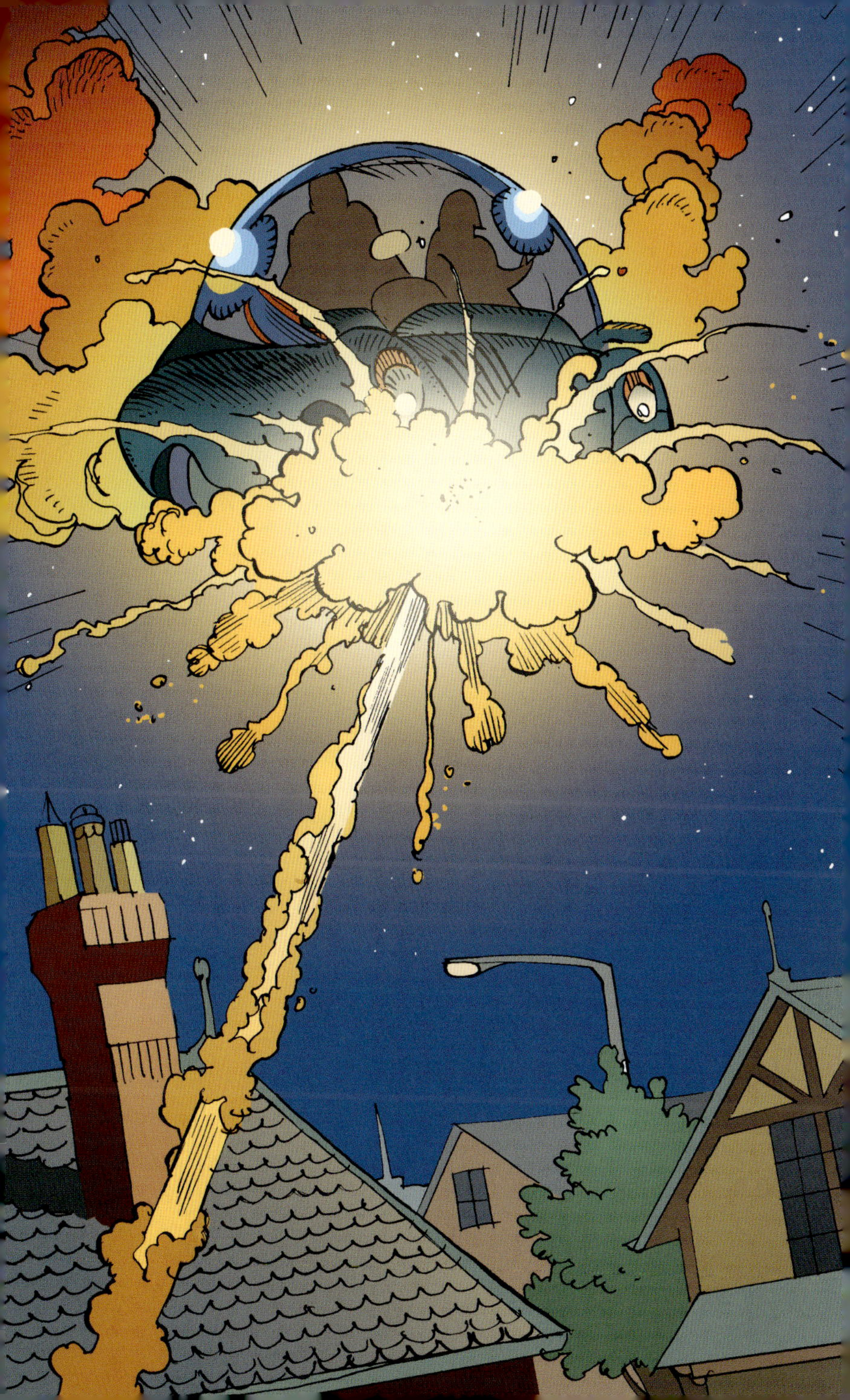

CHAPTER 13

Frankie threw up his arms as the fiery blast sent him spiralling through the air.

"Megan! Megan, where are you?" he screamed, but his voice was whipped away on the wind. The glare of the explosion was still imprinted on his eyeballs, but if he squinted he could just make out some clouds, some stars, and not a whole lot else.

He flipped and spun as he tumbled through the empty space. His ears were ringing from the blast. It was the only thing drowning out the howling wind as he plummeted down towards the city.

It spread out beneath him like an illuminated map. As Frankie fell, he spotted Megan. She was about fifty metres below, plunging backwards towards the Earth, her body flapping limply.

"Megan!" Frankie shouted. "Megan, wake up!"

Twisting in mid-air, he angled himself towards her. By tucking his arms in by his sides, Frankie was able to speed up. The wind tore at his face and clothes. It swirled up his nose and brought tears to his eyes, but still he kept falling, faster and faster, gaining on Megan with every moment.

They were barely above the highest rooftops now. Even over the roaring of the wind, Frankie could hear the sounds of the city below.

He reached out for Megan. Her eyes were closed, her face stained with soot. With a desperate grab, Frankie caught hold of her wrist. He pulled her towards him and wrapped himself around her, angling himself so his back was towards the fast-approaching pavement.

"Megan!" he yelped. "Wake up!"

Megan opened her eyes. She muttered below her breath, and a split second later they hit the ground with a *BOOM!*

The impact cracked the tarmac and shattered windows in every direction. For a moment, Frankie thought he had gone blind, until he realised his eyes were screwed tightly shut.

He opened his eyes to see a sphere of pink energy surrounding Megan and him, like a big protective bubble.

"H-hey, I did it," Megan said, as the wall of the bubble fizzled and then vanished. "We're alive."

"Speak for yourself," Frankie replied.

"You may be alive for now, little lady," drawled a horribly familiar voice. Frankie and Megan looked up in time to see Professor King drop a still-smoking missile launcher onto the pavement. "But I wouldn't get used to it if I were you."

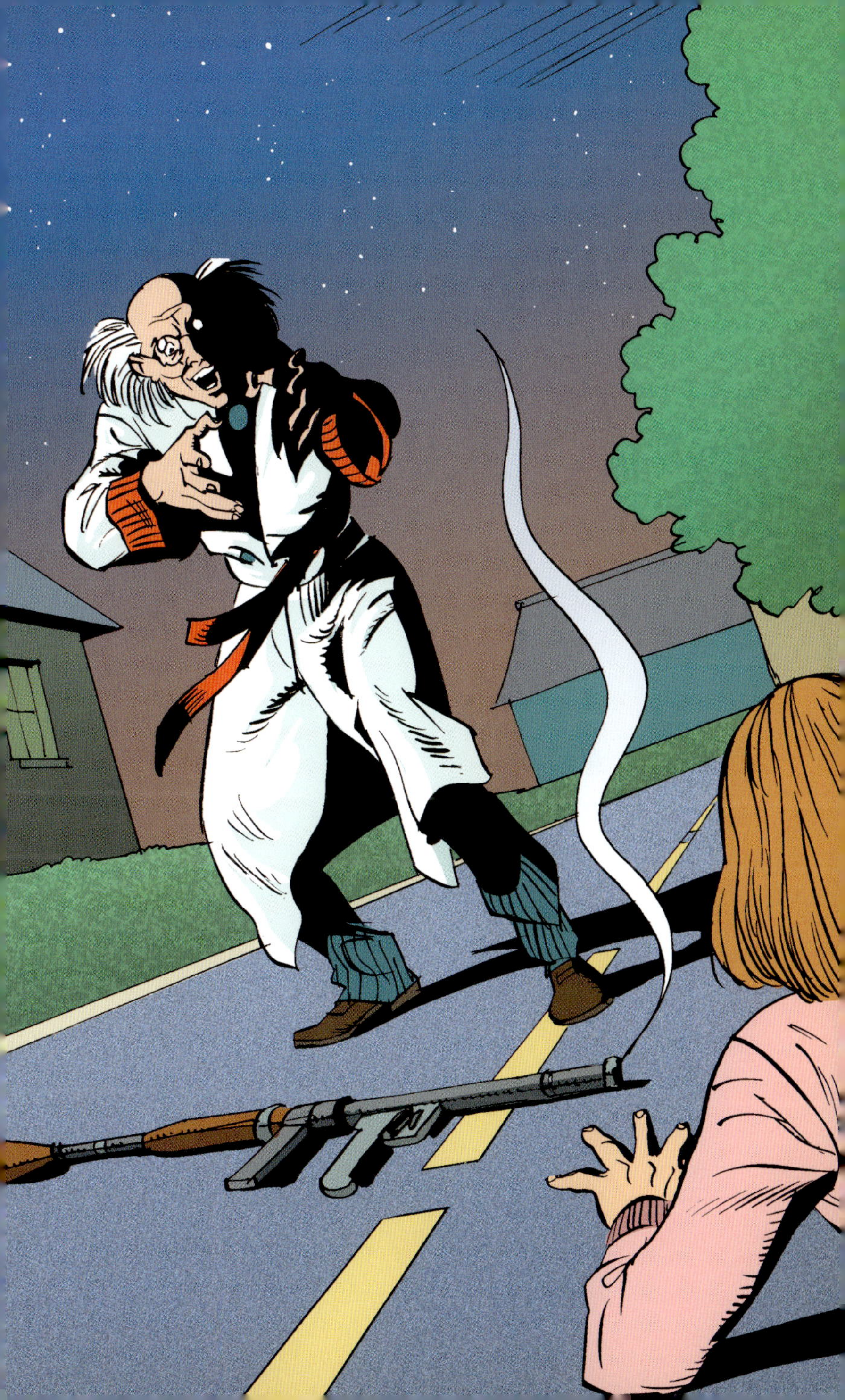

CHAPTER 14

Megan sprang to her feet. It took Frankie a little longer to peel himself off the pavement. His bones *cricked* and *cracked* as he straightened up.

"I hope you ain't damaged that body too badly," warned Professor King. "I want it back in one piece."

"Stay back," Megan warned. "You're not getting him. It's over, King. SPOOK's taking you down."

A sneer creased King's squashed-up little nose. "That's *my* monster, lady, and I'm taking him back."

"No," said Frankie. "You aren't."

He grabbed the professor by the front of his lab coat and hoisted him easily into the air.

"Wait, son! Stop, put me down. Come on, man!"

With a grunt, Frankie tossed the professor several metres across the road. The villain skidded across the cracked tarmac, then clattered to a clumsy stop.

Megan took out her badge. "Alvin King, by the authority of SPOOK, I am placing you under arrest. You have the right to remain ..."

"You think I'm that dumb?" King sniggered. "I'm a mad scientist. You think I wasn't ready for this?"

Thrusting a hand into his inside pocket, King brought out a test tube with a small cork in the top. A yellowy-green liquid bubbled and frothed inside.

Popping out the cork, the professor knocked back the potion in one gulp. There was a gurgling from deep inside him, then King threw back his head and let out a scream. His limbs shuddered and shook as pain coursed through his body. His eyes met Frankie's, and Frankie realised that, despite his agony, the professor was grinning.

RRRRIP!

The back of King's coat split open, revealing a back covered in hundreds of small sharp spikes. His arms bulged, his muscles tearing free of his sleeves.

Talon-like claws burst through the front of his shoes as his whole body began to grow. Megan and Frankie took a step backwards.

"He's taken some sort of mutant potion," Megan said. "He's making himself into a monster."

King hurled his fists to the sky and let out a roar. Most of his clothes now hung off him in scraps. He was three times as tall as he had been, and several times as wide. Scales and spikes stuck out of him in every direction. He towered above Frankie, and as he turned his gaze Frankie's way, madness blazed behind his eyes.

"Now," growled the professor, his teeth grinding together. "Who's first?"

Megan brought up both arms. Her hands twitched and fire flew from her fingertips. A ball of flame exploded across King's face.

"Tickles," he said, then he raised a knee to his chest and drove his foot down onto the ground.

With an ear-shattering *crack,* the surface of the road split open. With a scream, Megan tumbled down into the darkness, out of sight.

"Ding dong," King laughed. "The witch is dead."

"Megan!" Frankie cried. He made a dive for the crack, but a hand caught him by the leg and flicked him sharply upwards.

For a moment Frankie thought King was throwing him away, but then he felt himself returning to Earth with a sudden jerk.

BOOM! The professor slammed Frankie hard against the pavement.

"That body's my property," he roared, raising Frankie above his head again. "I'm taking it back, son, and there's nothing you can do to stop me!"

With a wild grab, Frankie caught hold of the professor's hair. Two large clumps of it came away in his hands, and King let out a wail of pain.

Frankie kicked free of the professor's grip and rolled clumsily to his feet.

"My hair, man!" bellowed King. "You ruined my beautiful hair."

With a roar, the professor lunged. Frankie ducked, then drove a punch into the monster's ribcage. It was like hitting a brick wall, and Frankie felt at least two of his knuckles shatter like glass.

A crunching backhand sent Frankie spinning to the pavement. Stars danced before his eyes. He tried to get up, but his brain felt as if it were about to trickle out through his ears.

A large shadow loomed above him. Frankie turned to see King standing there, a car raised above his head.

Frankie's eyes went wide. He swallowed nervously.

"Oh," he mumbled. "Bum."

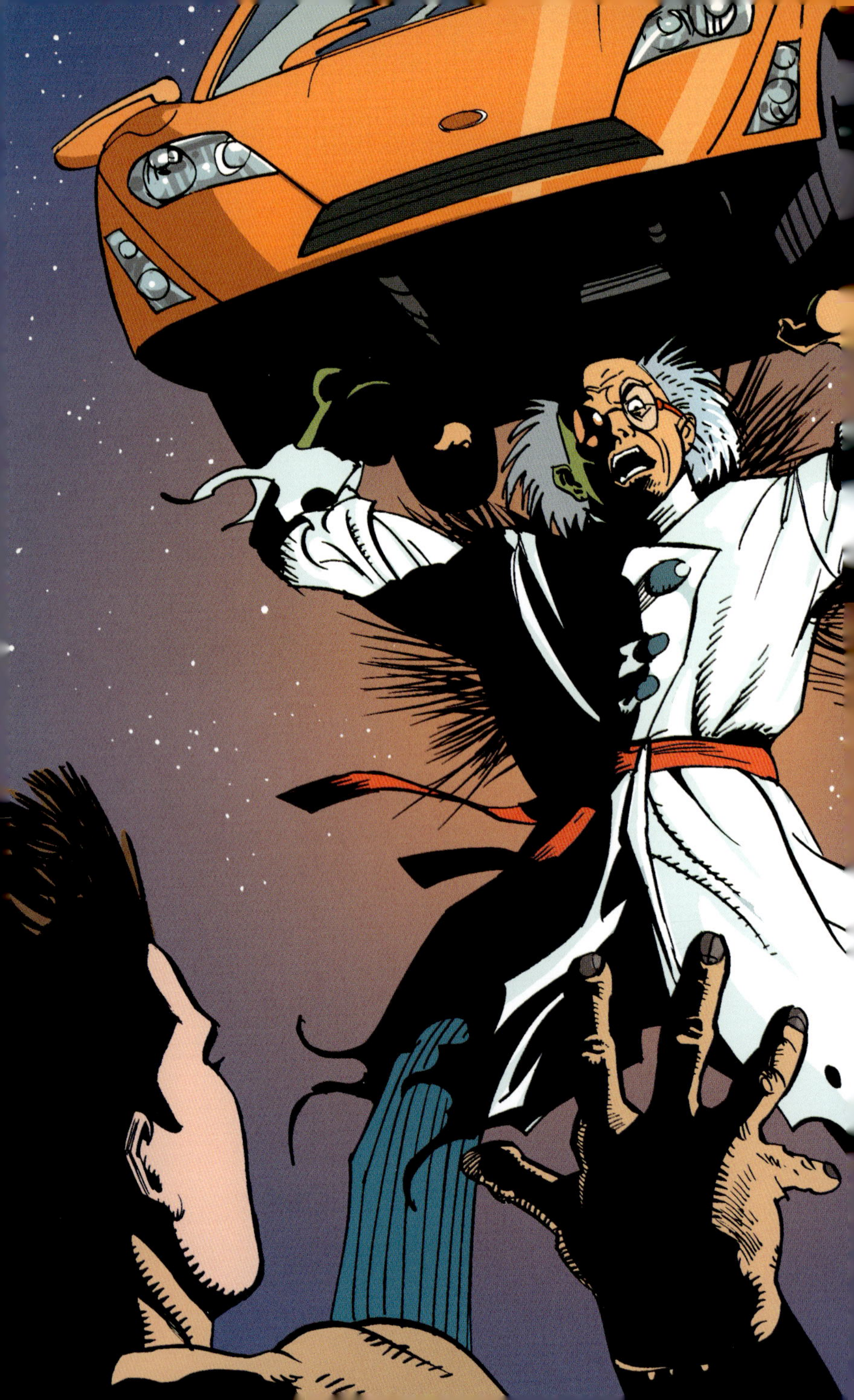

CHAPTER 15

Frankie scrambled for safety. Too late! The car crashed down on his back. The impact buckled his arms and pinned him to the pavement.

"And stay down," warned King. "I'm taking you home."

"N-not so fast," came a voice. Megan heaved herself up from the crack in the ground and got shakily to her feet. "You're not t-taking him."

"And who's going to stop me?"

From below the car Frankie saw flashes of light as Megan opened fire with every trick she had left. He heard King's sickening snigger and felt the ground shake as King made a grab for Megan.

"It's all in my head. There is no pain," Frankie whispered.

His arms were probably broken, but he pressed his palms against the ground and braced his back against the underside of the car. "*There is no pain!*"

He pushed upwards, his huge muscles straining to their limit. The metal groaned as the car began to tip. With one final effort Frankie rolled the car onto its side. King's head whipped around, and his eyes narrowed in rage.

"I told you to stay down!"

There was a street light just a few metres away. Frankie wrapped both hands around the bottom and pulled. The metal pole tore free from the ground just as King made a lunge for Frankie.

Frankie swung with the lamp post.

CLANG!

It crunched against King's jaw, sending him spinning. The professor hissed in animal rage and lunged again.

Frankie took another swing with the lamp post, but King was too quick. He ducked beneath it, then smacked the street light from Frankie's grip.

"Megan!" Frankie yelled. "Bubble us!"

"Got it!" With a flick of her fingers, Megan surrounded Frankie and King with a ball of magical energy. It distracted the professor just long enough for Frankie to twist up onto his back. He wrapped his hands around the monster's throat.

"Pathetic!" King barked. "This won't hold me for long!"

"Doesn't have to," Frankie replied. "Just long enough for the air to run out."

The professor's face fell. "No," he snarled. "No, you can't!"

"Oh, but I can," said Frankie. "I'm dead remember? Breathing's not on my list of priorities. I'm guessing it's pretty high up on yours."

Frankie squeezed. The professor sank down, gasping for breath, but the air inside the bubble was already getting thin.

Beneath Frankie, the monster began to shrink. The scaly and spiky back became smooth. The brutish body became skinny and thin.

"I … built … you," King wheezed, as he slumped onto the shimmering floor of the bubble.

"Maybe," said Frankie. "But I knocked you down."

The bubble popped out of existence, and Megan threw her arms around Frankie's waist. Or, at least, as far around it as she could reach.

"The police will be coming," she said. "We should clear out."

Frankie shook his head and lumbered away from her. "No," he said. "I'm going home. I've got to see my mum and dad."

And with that, he pushed past her and began to run.

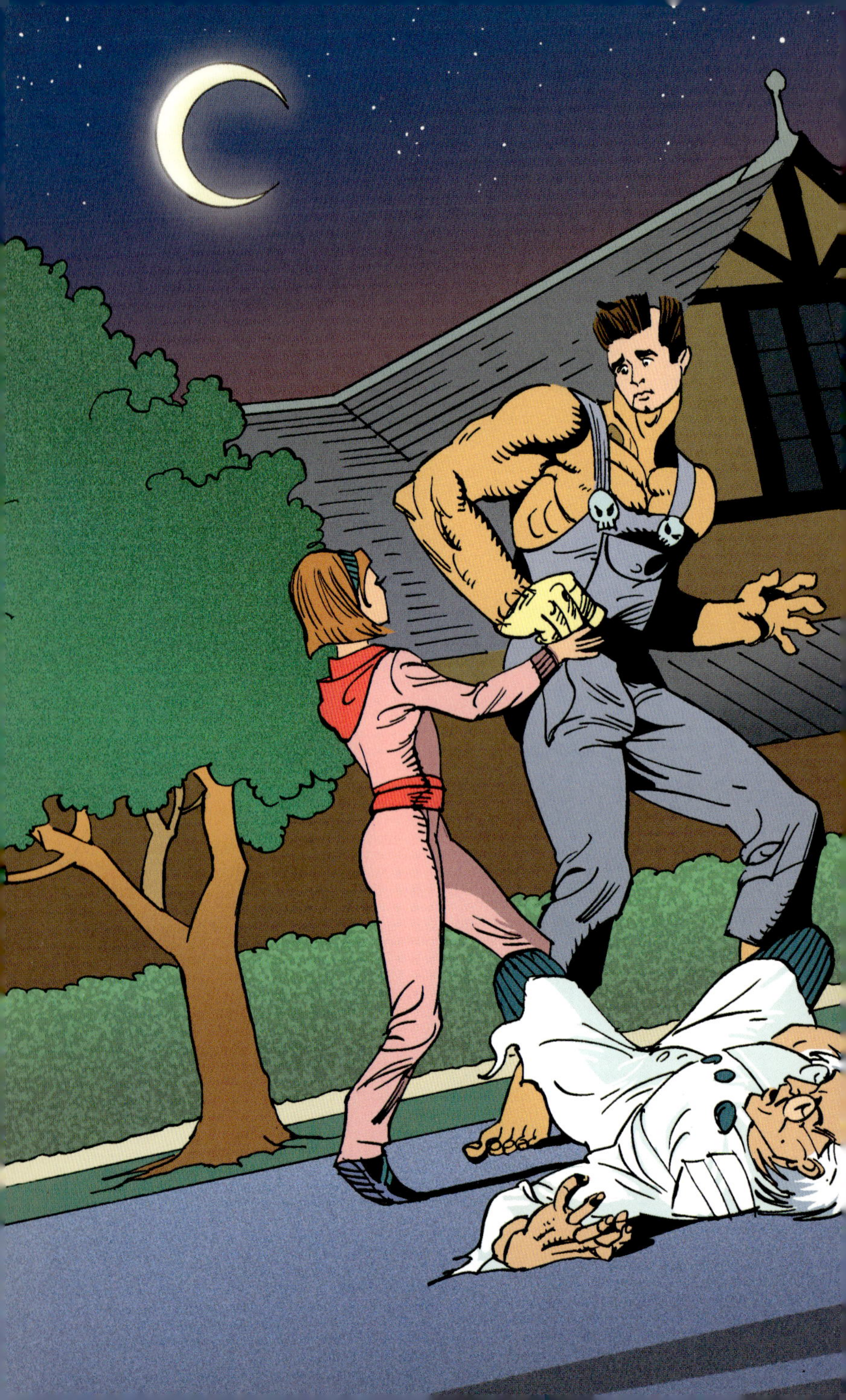

CHAPTER 16

"Frankie, wait!" Megan cried, but Frankie wasn't listening.

He bounded along familiar streets. He leaped over fences he'd climbed a hundred times before, past the shop, past the park, past the houses where his friends lived.

And then there it was, right in front of him – the living-room window of his family's ground-floor flat.

Home.

And there, sitting in their usual chairs, were his parents.

Only … Only …

"They're smiling," Frankie said. "They're … laughing."

Megan appeared behind him. He barely felt her hand on his arm.

"I tried to tell you, Frankie," she said. "Thing is … you've been dead for over eight years."

Frankie felt as if he was going to be sick. "And what … they've forgotten me?"

"Never," Megan told him. "They'll never forget you. They'll never get over what happened. But they're getting on with it, you know?"

"But … But I want to go home."

"I know," Megan said. "But what then? What sort of life would you be dooming them to? Hiding you in the cupboard whenever anyone comes round, scared someone will come to take you away."

She gave his arm a squeeze. "They're dealing with it. Scars heal. Even the really bad ones."

Frankie looked down at her, then at his mismatched body. "I can't let them see me, can I? Not like this."

Megan shook her head. "Sorry."

"So … what do I do?" he asked. "Where do I go?"

"Funny you should ask," Megan said.

She flipped open a black leather wallet, revealing a shiny silver badge and an ID card that read:

FRANKIE STINE, Agent of SPOOK

"You in?" Megan asked.

Frankie looked at the badge, then back to his house. He watched his dad reach over and give his mum's hand a squeeze. At last, he smiled and turned away.

"I'm in," he said, taking the wallet.

Megan patted him on the back. "Glad to hear it, partner," she said. "Now let's get King taken care of. Then we've got a new assignment. There's some weird travelling ghost train around. Lots of kids going missing."

"Sounds like a case for the Supernatural Police Officers OK," Frankie said. And he turned his back on the place where he had once lived, and walked with his new friend into the dark.

Reader challenge

Word hunt

1. On page 10, find an adjective that means "creepy" or "ghostly".

2. On page 33, find a noun that means "fairness".

3. On page 65, find a verb that means "pounced" or "dived".

Story sense

4. Why was Alvin King trying to use a knock-out dart on Frankie? (pages 14–18)

5. What did Frankie think when Megan first told him she was a witch who worked for SPOOK? (pages 27–34)

6. Why was Frankie not happy about being in the Dragonfly with Megan? (pages 46–54)

7. Give some examples of words or phrases used to describe King as he turns into a monster. (pages 61–63)

Your views

8. What did you think of the three main characters in the story (Frankie, Megan and King)?

9. How do you think Frankie felt when he realised he could never go home? Give reasons. (pages 74–76)

Spell it

With a partner, look at these words and then cover them up.

- see-through
- double-decker
- criss-crossed
- knock-out

Take it in turns for one of you to read the words aloud. The other person has to try and spell each word. Check your answers, then swap over.

Try it

Sit opposite a partner and play a game of verbal tennis. Take it in turns to think of a word or phrase to describe the character of Frankie Stine. Each person should give their response as quickly as possible. The first person to run out of ideas, or repeat something that has already been said, loses the game.

William Collins's dream of knowledge for all began with the publication of his first book in 1819. A self-educated mill worker, he not only enriched millions of lives, but also founded a flourishing publishing house. Today, staying true to this spirit, Collins books are packed with inspiration, innovation and practical expertise. They place you at the centre of a world of possibility and give you exactly what you need to explore it.

Collins. Freedom to teach.

Published by Collins Education
An imprint of HarperCollins Publishers
77-85 Fulham Palace Road
Hammersmith
London
W6 8JB

Browse the complete Collins Education catalogue at **www.collins.co.uk**

Text © Barry Hutchison 2014
Illustrations © Eoin Covenay 2014

Series consultants: Alan Gibbons and Natalie Packer

10 9 8 7 6 5 4 3 2 1
ISBN 978-0-00-754624-4

All rights reserved. No part of this publication may be reproduced, stored in a retrieval system, or transmitted in any form or by any means, electronic, mechanical, photocopying, recording or otherwise, without the prior written permission of the Publisher or a licence permitting restricted copying in the United Kingdom issued by the Copyright Licensing Agency Ltd, 90 Tottenham Court Road, London W1T 4LP.

British Library Cataloguing in Publication Data.
A catalogue record for this publication is available from the British Library.

Commissioned by Catherine Martin
Edited by Sue Chapple
Project-managed by Lucy Hobbs and Caroline Green
Illustration management by Tim Satterthwaite
Proofread by Hugh Hillyard-Parker
Typeset by Jouve India, Ltd
Production by Emma Roberts
Printed and bound in China by South China Printing Co.
Cover design by Paul Manning

Acknowledgements

The publishers would like to thank the students and teachers of the following schools for their help in trialling the *Read On* series:

Parkview Academy, London
Southfields Academy, London
St Mary's College, Hull
Queensbury School, Queensbury, Bradford
Ormiston Six Villages Academy, Chichester